ISBN: 978-1-951428-13-6

First printed edition 2020

The Angelic Prince Publishing Company
PO Box 33572
Tulsa, OK 74153

Brilliant Words For Brilliant Kids

Brilliant Words For Brilliant Kids

Intro

YOU DON'T HAVE TO SCORE REAL HIGH ON AN IQ TEST TO PROVE YOU'RE SMART. SOMETIMES ALL IT TAKES IS THE RIGHT WORD SAID AT THE RIGHT TIME FOR PEOPLE TO RECOGNIZE HOW INTELLIGENT YOU REALLY ARE.

JOIN HIS ROYAL HIGHNESS KING LO TEE BUGG KAI LING; THE WEALTHIEST DOG IN THE WORLD AS HE HELPS EXPAND YOUR VOCABULARY WHILE YOU ENJOY FUN ILLUSTRATIONS THAT TEACH 'Brilliant Words For Brilliant Kids'.

TO GET THE MOST OUT OF THIS BOOK YOU WILL BE GIVEN THE DEFINITION OF EACH NEW WORD AS WELL AS 4 POSSIBLE WAYS OF CORRECTLY USING IT.

Brilliant Words For Brilliant Kids

Dynamic

Dye-nam-ick

1. A positive attitude, full of energy and new ideas

2. Can be seen as an activity which shows a constant change of progress or growth

Brilliant Words For Brilliant Kids

I make sure I am dynamic in everything I do.

The food at this restaurant is amazing and their executive chef is dynamic!

The world will always be in need of more dynamic leaders. Don't afraid to be one of them.

I will do all I can to lead a dynamic life.

Brilliant Words For Brilliant Kids

Diligence

dill-uh-gents

1. To do something persistently with care

2. A steady, earnest, energetic effort to get a task done quickly

Brilliant Words For Brilliant Kids

Do everything with diligence.

The gift of diligence is success.

The difference between a mediocre-ordinary life and an extraordinary one is that one is led by diligence while the other is not.

It is very simple to understand... diligence is the complete opposite of laziness.

Brilliant Words For Brilliant Kids

Allegiance

uh-lee-jence

1. A commitment of loyalty to a worthy individual, group or a cause

2. The pledge of fidelity owed by a citizen of a sovereign government in exchange for the country's management and protection of the citizen

Brilliant Words For Brilliant Kids

Saying the pledge of allegiance is your sworn vow that you love, support and would defend your country.

Being loyal is the most important thing to those who have made a sworn allegiance.

I will do everything I can to help and protect my family. My allegiance will always be to those I love the most.

Every citizen should be grateful to be living in a FREE, safe and thriving country. When citizens have all these things... allegiance is easy.

Brilliant Words For Brilliant Kids

Character

Care-eck-tor

1. The mental behaviors and moral qualities acted out which become the distinctive identity of an individual

2. Two distinct types of characters exist; good and bad

Brilliant Words For Brilliant Kids

When you are around people with a good character, you will always have a good time. When you are around people of bad character, you won't.

He was fun to around because his character is larger than life.

Shady characters will always give you the creeps.

I am proud to be a person of good character. I am nice, respectful, honest, kind and caring.

Brilliant Words For Brilliant Kids

Exceed

X-seed

1. To go beyond the limits

2. To excel and surpass others, an advancement into superior levels

Brilliant Words For Brilliant Kids

I do all I can to do my best to exceed everyone's expectations of what I can accomplish.

It is always safest to not exceed the speed limits.

That movie was better than I thought. It completely exceeded my expectations.

I want my life to exceed my greatest dreams.

Brilliant Words For Brilliant Kids

Serene

Sir-Eeen

1. A term of respect made to members of royal families such as a title of dignity E.g. 'Your Serene Royal Highness'.

2. A state of tranquility, one who is untroubled, a feeling of peace and calm at all times especially when under pressure

Brilliant Words For Brilliant Kids

She is serene as a queen full of grace. She is always beautifully calm and composed at all times. Nothing worries her so that empowers her.

The stunning sunsets over Table Rock Lake are astoundingly serene.

Serene people are extremely confident as they are in command of everything including themselves. This virtue allows them to naturally remain calm and smile at all times.

The epitome of true human achievement is the attainment of a happiness and tranquility which grants a serene and peaceful life.

Brilliant Words For Brilliant Kids

Confidence

Kon-fed-ence

1. The ability to believe you are quipped with enough God-given abilities to accomplish anything you put your mind and hands to

2. To feel or believe that you can trust or rely on someone

Brilliant Words For Brilliant Kids

Having confidence is a trait that EVERYONE ADMIRES!

Your are the keeper of your own flame. Let no one in life blow it out. It is your confidence. It is your belief that you are awesome and because of it you can do anything.

People who have confidence effortlessly command attention and turn heads without even trying wherever they go.

Make a commitment to yourself to become your own greatest fan and biggest supporter in life. This confidence helps lead you toward a happiness that those who don't have self-confidence will never understand.

Brilliant Words For Brilliant Kids

Excellence

X-sell-ence

1. The ability to be outstanding or extremely good at something

2. A skill, virtue or other valuable quality which makes you excellent

Brilliant Words For Brilliant Kids

Excellence is within everyone's reach. It is in knowing that you did your very best.

Make excellence a habit and watch good things come your way.

Practice makes perfect which means the more you do it the closer you get to excellence.

When people think of you... make them think of excellence.

Brilliant Words For Brilliant Kids

Perseverance

purr-sev-Ear-ents

1. The ability to not give up, give in, or stop when confronting difficulty

2. The ability to see obstacles simply as temporary delays or detours to achieving success

Brilliant Words For Brilliant Kids

Those who've climbed the tallest mountains exhibit the most perseverance.

People with perseverance always look back on difficult times and smile, and are ever grateful they did not let anything stop them.

Success belongs to those who have self-confidence and perseverance.

Perseverance allows you to see past an impossible situation until it is behind you.

Brilliant Words For Brilliant Kids

Trustworthy

trust-wurr-ThEE

1. Someone you trust who is good, loyal, honest, dependable, solid, tried-and-true

2. Those who wish to see that you are protected and safe

Brilliant Words For Brilliant Kids

Be trustworthy and find friends who are also trustworthy.

If you get a really weird feeling in your stomach when you meet a person... they most likely are NOT trustworthy.

Dogs are one of the most trustworthy creatures known to man.

Being trustworthy is an important virtue. It can lead to greater opportunities and responsibilities in life.

Brilliant Words For Brilliant Kids

AchiEvement

uh-cheeve-ment

1. A successful accomplishment attained through effort, courage or skill which could be honored with distinction

2. A remarkable, great or heroic deed

Brilliant Words For Brilliant Kids

Never stop achieving. Achievements are one of the greatest pleasures in life.

Each achievement is your certification that you put your skills to great use.

Be patient. Achievement takes effort which requires time.

Great achievements usually follow those who have had high expectations in life. Those who dream BIG GET MORE!

Brilliant Words For Brilliant Kids

Tenacious

ten-Aye-shous

1. Persistence, not easily stopped or pulled apart, adhering to or seeking something of value

2. One who has the focus and determination to relentlessly stay strong and firm to continue until the very end

Brilliant Words For Brilliant Kids

You don't have to be the smartest, strongest or best looking to succeed as long as you are tenacious. Rewards are never given to those who quit.

If you are tenacious, no one can talk you out of, sidetrack you, derail you or stop you from achieving your goals. Tenacity is the tracks leading you to what you want.

Don't just chase dreams. Be strong and tenacious to see they come true.

All it takes is a STRONG WILL to be tenacious. The tenacious are unstoppable!

Brilliant Words For Brilliant Kids

Admiration

add-murr-Aye-shun

1. Occurs when someone is impressed by a person who has accomplished a great act or respect-worthy feat

2. Held to a level of respect and great esteem

Brilliant Words For Brilliant Kids

Your dog's love is so great for you. Most times you never realize how much they look at you through eyes of complete admiration.

The world will always have great admiration for Michael Angelo for his amazing life's work.

"The love of family and the admiration of friends is much more important than wealth and privilege." Charles Kuralt

Don't live in hopes of admiration, but if you get it... enjoy it.

Brilliant Words For Brilliant Kids

Captivate

cap-teh-Vate

1. Irresistible appeal with beauty and charm

2. The ability to mesmerize and hold your attention

Brilliant Words For Brilliant Kids

The true aim of an artist is to captivate his audience.

An astounding, impressive, awe-inspiring performance puts the audience in a trance which captivates them.

From the first moment I saw her she took my breath away. She seemed to captivate everyone who saw her as she walked by.

The mermaids were able to captivate the sailors with their beauty and alluring songs.

Brilliant Words For Brilliant Kids

Accomplishment

uh-com-pliSH-ment

1. A successful achievement of a task

2. A skillful activity which is the result of extreme study or practice.

Brilliant Words For Brilliant Kids

Use every talent you've been given to achieve every accomplishment in your life.

Your greatest accomplishment in life will be being yourself while living in a world trying to make you into something you were never meant to be.

Each and every accomplishment starts with your decision to try.

"Nothing builds self-esteem and self-confidence like accomplishment." Thomas Carlyle

Brilliant Words For Brilliant Kids

Resiliency

re-zill-yen-see

1. The ability to become strong, healthy, or successful again after something bad has happened; the capacity to recover from difficulties

2. The ability of a substance or object to spring back into shape after it has been smashed or deformed.

Brilliant Words For Brilliant Kids

Resiliency is your ability to overcome the unexpected. Whatever difficulties are thrown to you in life, know that nothing will ever stop you because you always bounce back better than ever.

I was born with extreme resiliency to bounce-back from anything.

Resiliency whispers in your ear to not be afraid. She tries to remind you... YOU WILL WIN IN THE END. The problem is her voice is so faint most people do not hear her, but those who do bounce back from everything.

My resiliency is greater than I realize. I always find a way to come back stronger.

Brilliant Words For Brilliant Kids

AdEpt

uh-Dept

1. A person of great knowledge and aptitude with experience who is extremely skilled or proficient at something

2. Implies a dexterity executed with expert skills that perform at perfect levels every time; an advanced master in any art, occupation or trade.

Brilliant Words For Brilliant Kids

Adepts know the importance of remaining calm, while under pressure, to focus their skills on the task at hand.

Martial art adepts remain calm in fights to become fierce weapons.

If you aspire to become an adept, you will at least become your very best.

Some people are more intelligent than others because they are more adept in certain areas.

Brilliant Words For Brilliant Kids

Genuine

jenn-U-en

1. Truly is what something is said to be; authentic

2. An emotion or action of a person done in sincerity

Brilliant Words For Brilliant Kids

Being genuine is being who you are and loving it.

People can tell when you are fake or if you are genuine. Everyone loves genuine people and hates fakes. There is no doubt... IT IS A WIN-WIN TO BE GENUINE.

When you apologize, be genuine and sincere when you say it. Make the person know that you meant it.

The coolest people are those who are happy, good and genuine.

Brilliant Words For Brilliant Kids

Dignity

dig-ne-tee

1. A sense of pride and self respect

2. A manner, style, state or quality worthy of honor or respect, possessing an air of high, noble or honorable rank of position

Brilliant Words For Brilliant Kids

The sense of stateliness, nobility, majesty, regality and grandeur are the best choice of words to describe the truest definition of dignity.

"An identity without dignity is wasted." Lantz de Contreras

"Dignity is the result of self-respect and self-esteem sparking in sync." Lantz de Contreras

Never sacrifice three things:
Your heart
Your family
Your dignity

Brilliant Words For Brilliant Kids

Noteworthy

Note-were-thee

1. Worthy of attracting attention for being interesting, significant or exhibiting an unusual level of special excellence

2. Something of remarkable importance or interesting enough to be noticed or receive attention

Brilliant Words For Brilliant Kids

"A noteworthy life is attained by those who make an effort to lead one." Lantz de Contreras

You never forget seeing a noteworthy performance.

Be remarkable and you will become noteworthy.

Noteworthy: The ability to be noticed for doing things significantly outstanding.

Brilliant Words For Brilliant Kids

Ingenuity

Engine-new-ity

1. The quality of being clever, original, creative innovative and inventive

2. Ingenious; being able to think outside of the box

Brilliant Words For Brilliant Kids

All of the greatest moments in history sprang from ingenuity.

Every problem can be solved with a little ingenuity.

Ingenuity will always first appear as a hunch that you can't get out of your mind until you see if the idea is correct.

A little ingenuity can make you wealthy.

Enchanting Books Which Make Readers of Every Age More Brilliant
The King Lo Tee Bugg Brilliant Book Series
What Happens When Puppies Pray
Ages 1-8
Making of a King
Ages 1-8
The World's Greatest Coloring Book! Coloring Book 1
Ages 2-12
The World's Greatest Coloring Book! Coloring Book 2
Ages 2-12
His Royal Highness King Lo Tee Bugg Kalling's Royal Big Top Circus Coloring Book 1
Ages 2-12
His Royal Highness King Lo Tee Bugg Kalling's Royal Farm Book 1
Ages 2-12
His Royal Highness King Lo Tee Bugg Kalling's Royal Big Top Circus Coloring Book 2
Ages 2-12
His Royal Highness King Lo Tee Bugg Kalling's Royal Farm Coloring Book 2
Ages 2-12
Safari
Ages 4-12
Ages 6-10
Safari Coloring Book 1
Ages 2-12
What Happens When Puppies Pray
Ages 8-Adult
Brilliant Minds Won't Cuss! Cool Swearing Alternatives
Brilliant Minds Won't Cuss! 2
Ages 7-13
Brilliant Words For Brilliant Kids
Brilliant Words For Brilliant Kids 2
Ages 8-Adult

HOPE FOR TODAY AND TOMORROW
SHORT MEANINGFUL MESSAGES VOL. 1
HOPE FOR TODAY AND TOMORROW
SHORT MEANINGFUL MESSAGES VOL. 2
ADULT COLORING PROJECTS
PEACE AND TRANQUILITY
ADULT COLORING PROJECTS
Jollification
See Every Page of Every Book For Free at
LANTZ DECONTRERAS .COM
MY AMAZING BOOK OF MAZES
INSPRIATIONAL QUOTES AND COLORING PROJECTS
LANTZ DE CONTRERAS
SUPERNATURAL FAVOR
LANTZ DECONTRERAS
WRATH MERCILESS EX
LANTZ DECONTRERAS
THE ANGELIC FORNICATION SERIES
THE GATHERING
LANTZ DECONTRERAS
SCAN ME
FLOWCODE
PRIVACY.FLOWCODE.COM
THE GAME OF KINGS
ADULT COLOURING BOOK
1
GAME OF KINGS
2
Brilliant Words For Brilliant Minds
The Adult and Young Adult Collection

Become a
SUPERFAN
and Instantly DOWNLOAD
FREE GIFTS
FOR YOU and YOUR FAMILY!
12 FREE
PRINTABLE COLORING PAGES
AND 12 FREE PRINTABLE COLOR POSTERS
Do grand things!
Be brilliant!
Be Excellent!
LANTZ
DECONTRERAS
.COM

PLUS: A 5-WEEK EMAIL COURSE REVEALING
'THE MYSTERIES OF THE ANGELIC REALMS'

IN THE NEXT 5 WEEKS
YOU WILL LEARN:

You Have a Guardian Angel
The Number of Angels
The Hierarchy, Choirs and Nations of Angels
Every Angel Has a Name
The Appearance of Angels
The Speed of Angels
The Songs of Angels
The Strength of Angels
The Language of Angels
The Gender of Angels
The Height of Angels
The Children of Angels; the Nephilim
The History of the Birthday Cake and Angels

Be sure to watch for Lantz's Uplifting emails.

TO RECEIVE YOUR FREE GIFTS

SCAN ME

FLOWCODE

PRIVACY.FLOWCODE.COM

Go to:

HTTPS://WWW.LANTZDECONTRERAS.COM/FAMILY-GIFT-BONUS.HTML

Printed in Great Britain
by Amazon

44878598R00030